A soulful surrender

Elizabeth Gutierrez

BookLeaf Publishing

Presentation by *BookLeaf Publishing*

Web: www.bookleafpub.com

E-mail: info@bookleafpub.com

ISBN: 9789357441018

First edition 2023

ACKNOWLEDGEMENT

I would like to acknowledge a special someone who made me realize that it is okay to be vulnerable.

Theft

I want to steal.
Not possessions or money
If time is the most valuable resource
I want to steal your time
Because every moment with you is
Worth more than any possession I could ever
have
My god, I want to steal.

End of The Road

If I'd had known that our last time would be the
end of the road for us...
I would have held you a little tighter,
and kissed you a little longer.

Gaslit

You can feel it
Permeating the room
Your senses heightened
"Nothing is going on."
But the room gets hotter and hotter
And the smell continues to pervade the room
You can feel it...
But it isn't until you light the match
That the room explodes

It can never be

Skin to skin
We lay here
I catch a glimpse of you looking
at me
Instead of breaking your gaze
I hold it
Getting lost in your blue eyes and
yours in mine
Both of us coming to understand the same thing
That these moments are for us now
But no matter how strong the connection
It can never be

Don't Stand too Close.

I often remember how it felt to have you hold
me
So warm, so tender
Your touch felt like fire
I was so cold, leaning on anything for warmth
I felt like I needed you to live
Until you burned me

Savor

I try to savor every moment I have
Understanding that each moment is fleeting
I will submerge myself in the
heartache, anger, love,
the happiness, the laughter, the sadness,
the excitement
Because each second
Each minute
Each hour
Each day
Each week
Each month
Each year
Passes and suddenly...
Those moments are gone
And I'm afraid if I don't savor
them, I won't remember them-
And I'll lose them, forgetting the
source of the feelings that make me
feel alive.

What is the Point?

Little is known about why we [humans] are here
Or anything for that matter
I often ponder what the point of anything is
Is it for each of us to simply live and die?
Is it for us to search for the meaning of life?
Is it for us to better understand each other?
Is it pointless?
In the grand scheme of things, none of us will
know.
No matter how we attempt to prolong our youth,
every human dies.
There will not be a detox, vegetable, exercise, or
lifestyle
that will make any of us survive death
It is all of our fate.
So again, what is the point of life?
To experience true love. true heartache. true loss.
To make mistakes. Fall. Be the hero and the
villain. To understand.
To comprehend and to misunderstand. To figure
most of it out.
And then die.

The Basement

The Basement
A forgotten place
Run down and overwhelmed

The Basement
Cold and cluttered
Filled with sadness and despair

The Basement
Traumatic memories fill the air
Locked up and forgotten
No one goes down there

My Basement
No one gets to see
It isn't until you come around
Willing to help me-

Unpack and declutter
Go through the complete mess

The Basement
My Basement
Filled with less distress

Here and Now

Time
Quickly passing us by
A sibling goes to prom
A friend gets married
I, myself, leave where I currently inhabit
Each of us stepping into a new role, or
environment
Forgetting that at one time
We felt that we were going through the hardest
parts of our lives

Life moves so quickly- we shift, we run towards,
we worry, we wait, we long for,
we-

are always moving and it is such a shame.
Such a shame that we are always looking
forward and what is to come next.
Or hoping for the next best thing.

When the best thing we can do is enjoy
what's happening, right here, right now
Because it's all we have

Loving Me

You were meant for me
You do the little things
The things I have always wanted done for me
Little notes, neck kisses, and remembering the
things I say in passing

You were meant for me
You support me and love me- each and every
angle
Every mood swing, and mismatch outfit

I don't know why I say it in the past tense
When you are right here in front of me
Pursuing me
Loving me for all that I am

You are meant for me
So I will lean in and embrace everything you
and I are
Perfection- no.
But real? yes.

Stop! You're Squeezing Me!

When do people decide what is worth it?
the effort-

When do people figure it out?
themselves out?

The dyeing, the plucking, the pricking, the
needles, and the scalpels
They'll say, "it's their life; let them live it"
But is it truly their [anyone's] decision?

When every magazine, screen, and video
Will continue to have their opinions permeate
your subconscious
scroll, scroll, switch to another platform
scroll, scroll, switch
It's been decided.

You'll get that haircut, buy that product, and live
"that" lifestyle
Or at least try

Try continuously, bit by bit
To try and
become "that"

Whatever it may look like

I can't decide if we ever really figure out who we
are
Or if we ever would
Without society's grip

Are you going to take a piece?

Fractions of life. Bits and bits and bits and bits.

Not all of us get to experience it all.

But many of us won't even ask for a piece.

Favorite Day of the Week

tuesdays.
pulling into the driveway
the garage wide open with-
oldies blaring on the stereo

tuesdays.
fresh cut grass
a guaranteed family dinner

tuesdays.
an attentive parent
a sense of normalness

until you'd leave

naked

I want to strip for you
strip every layer
down to my core
to show you
that I can be,
I am.
something more.

Nice girls can finish last too

to have your heart broken
is to know that you felt love

to fall down
is to know that you can get up, and walk away

to feel speechless
is to know that you can still have a voice

to be angry
is to know that you have passion

the true strength

Let betrayal and the hurt that comes with it be a reflection of the person who dealt it. Don't let your heart permeate in those feelings. While your heart may ache, your heart should not be tarnished due to their faults, but let it be an ode to your strength: being willing to open yourself up to be genuinely vulnerable.

Wear your Rain Boots

I can't cry because that'd make me weak

But with one drink and the blaring sound of a
song that hits the pressure points of my nerves

I'm gone, and the floodgates fill.

Let's go for a walk

It's such an incredibly beautiful thing when you
see someone you love find someone who
understands them.

Understanding their tendencies and when they
are ready to go home.

Understanding when they need a hug, a kiss, or
when they're upset.

Understanding that their person, their partner is
a product of their lived experience.

It's not beautiful because it's perfect-

It's beautiful because it's imperfect.

The beauty is found within the cracks of the
foundation that have had years of cement
pressed into it

And they're not there to fix it but to mend the
wear and tear of their lover's experiences

Making sure they're capable of yet another walk.

human

I'm at a crossroad
Between feeling everything or nothing at all

I've gone back and forth-
Between deciding to feel every moment,
every emotion that comes with each day,
each hardship, each heartbreak, each moment of
pure bliss

But sometimes, it hurts too much

I feel too much.

I think back to when I didn't allow
myself to feel anything. I was hollow-
avoiding any emotion, I was uncomfortable
with-
I've been growing to feel more at
ease with pain, hurt, sorrow- but then I wonder...

Does feeling everything and showing emotion
make me look weak?

Or does it make me human?

Red Car

I loved you when you had a red car
I remember the first drive in your car
When you played that song, that felt like it was
made just for us
The keychains dangling on the dash
I loved every second of that moment
That car is engrained in my memory
Etched like a carving on a tree
Every time I saw a red car, I
hoped that it'd be you
Also, looking for me in mine
But to my surprise, it was never you,
and I realize that
You'd probably be paying attention to the road,
not who might be in the car.
Which is why I almost hit that red car
Passing by

Telepathy

How special was it to look you in the eyes, say nothing, and feel heard

A feeling I had never experienced. I had been shouting my whole life, begging to be listened to and understood. Only for your soft eyes to lock with mine and share that you understood me, heard me, and saw me for exactly the person I was without a single exchange of words.